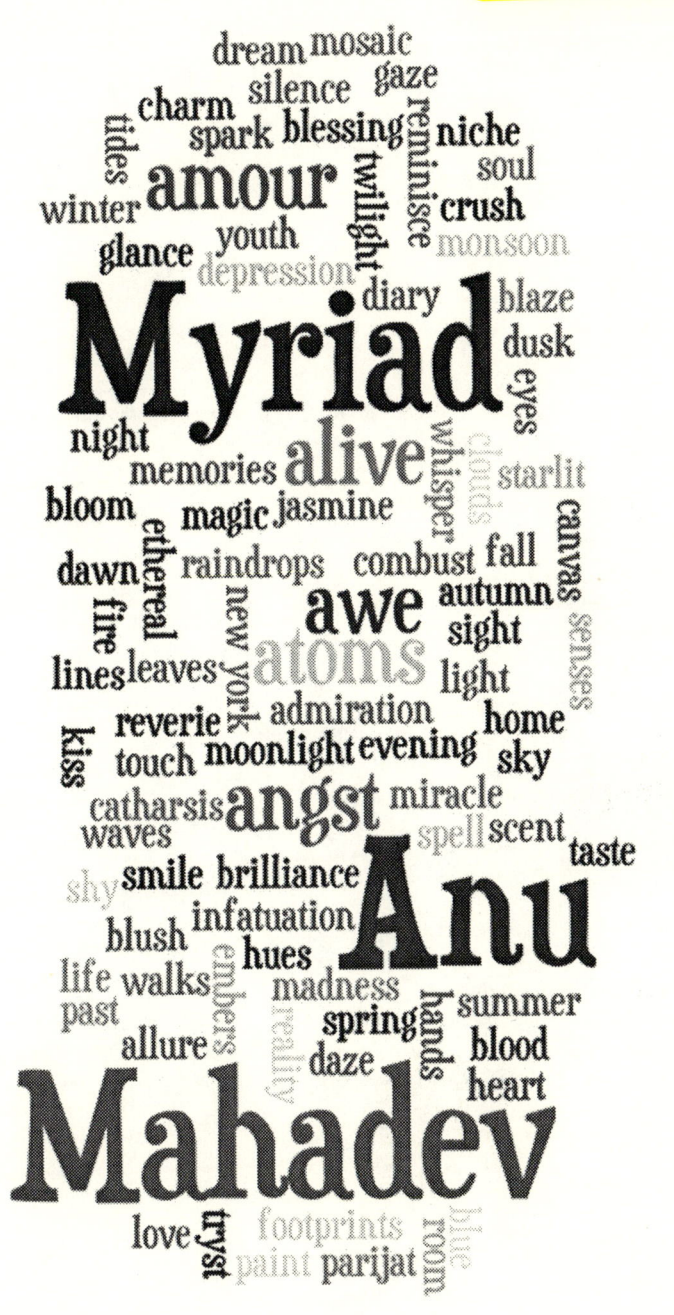

dream mosaic
charm silence gaze
tides spark blessing reminisce niche
winter amour soul
youth twilight crush
glance depression monsoon
diary blaze
Myriad dusk
eyes
night memories alive whisper starlit
bloom magic jasmine clouds canvas
dawn raindrops combust fall
ethereal awe autumn
fire atoms sight senses
lines leaves new york light
reverie admiration home
kiss touch moonlight evening sky
catharsis angst miracle
waves spell scent taste
shy smile brilliance
blush infatuation **Anu**
life walks hues embers
past allure madness hands summer
reality spring blood
daze heart
Mahadev
love tryst footprints blue
paint parijat room

authorHOUSE

AuthorHouse™
1663 Liberty Drive
Bloomington, IN 47403
www.authorhouse.com
Phone: 1-800-839-8640

© 2013 by Anu Mahadev. All rights reserved.

No part of this book may be reproduced, stored in a retrieval system, or transmitted by any means without the written permission of the author.

Published by AuthorHouse   01/15/2013

ISBN: 978-1-4817-0645-2 (sc)
ISBN: 978-1-4817-0644-5 (e)

Library of Congress Control Number: 2013900702

Any people depicted in stock imagery provided by Thinkstock are models, and such images are being used for illustrative purposes only.
Certain stock imagery © Thinkstock.

This book is printed on acid-free paper.

Because of the dynamic nature of the Internet, any web addresses or links contained in this book may have changed since publication and may no longer be valid. The views expressed in this work are solely those of the author and do not necessarily reflect the views of the publisher, and the publisher hereby disclaims any responsibility for them.

*Dear Nidhi,
enjoy the book!
Love,
Ann*

Dedicated to

My family and closest friends, without which neither this book nor this life would be possible.

Foreword

By

Deepa Sundararaman.

It is with pride, joy and a feeling of honor that I take this opportunity to introduce Anu's first book of poems to you.

My friendship with Anu is in its tenth year now, and relating how I know her is very telling about this lovely poet's personality. Anu is married to my husband's closest childhood friend. Many a friendship falls by the wayside when marriages happen and a new personality enters the mix, but no, this friendship only got stronger. She embraced their friendship, added to it and soon, she had "adopted" my husband to be her brother. A few years later, I enter the picture. Again, I give this strong woman all credit for warmly and enthusiastically including me into that friendship and today, I don't consider her my husband's sister or his friend's wife, but as my friend and confidante.

This book is categorized into five segments: awe, amour, angst, alive and a final segment of short poems called atoms. I've read them all and love them. And I hope you will too. As you read them, you will understand how they bring out joy, passion, pain, angst or wonder so expressively. When I read them, I felt as if her soul is in the poems, as if she personally experienced what her characters express.

Whether it be laughing to a joke, enjoying a crisp autumn day, disapproving of someone or something she doesn't like, taking pride in her son's latest achievement, being disappointed with something that didn't go right, there are no half measures for this girl. And that's exactly why her poems are such a beautiful read. She brings her heightened sensitivity into her work and I believe that helps her turn out such heartfelt poems.

Go on. I've said enough. Turn over the page and start experiencing . . .

Awe

Rose

Perhaps I was once a rose
That attracted bees and humans alike
And drove them insane with my scent
Perhaps I adorned a fair maiden's coif
Or was distilled into attar
And decorated a woman's boudoir
Perhaps I was a muse to an artist
Or a prop in a flower show
Or crushed under lovers' impatient feet
I am happy to have filled
So many lives
Who were not dissuaded by my thorns.

Fall

Pumpkin lattes and hearty soups
Fleece jackets and warm scarves
Apple picking and harvest festivals
Pies, squash and fresh corn bread
Orange colors splashed everywhere
Bird-watching and hay rides
Relaxing warmly in cozy blankets
Reading novels by the fire
Smell of spices in the air
Family gatherings in lamp lit rooms
Leaves blowing in the wind
Longer nights and shorter days
Quiet candle-lit dinners
Fall must be here after all!

Autumn Lovers

running anklets
crushing the shiuli
flowers underfoot
lovers' quarrel
gone awry
white dupatta
caught in the
jacaranda tree
gives a pause
as her clinking
silver bracelet
a gift from him
sparkles in the
glistening sun
as do her droplets
of mercurial tears
making her way
through beds of
zinnias and myrtle
fragrant as a flower
herself, she catches
up to her beloved
as the sharad ritu
enfolds around them
pleas and entreaties
ravishing poetry and
rash promises
amidst the heady scent
of the blossoms
and for that perfect
moment, all is right
in the world of the
paramours.

Turnover

No one accuses Fall
of letting go
too easily,
of unburdening
and moving on
without a thought
of shedding
those beautiful
leaves, those stories
collected over the year
without a care
of creating a canopy
of wasted experiences
If nature can do this
each year without regret,
or holding on
to those old clothes,
golden though they may be
then surely so can we?

Leaf

the leaf, detached
buoyed by the wind
drifted along the water
deposited on the banks
trampled by a child
buffeted again by the breeze
settled on a bower
drenched by the rains
buried by the snow
breathed her last sigh
became one with the earth
from whence she came.

The end of Fall

Lying lazily
on the leaves of
autumn; I quite
forget all those
mundane chores
I have to do.
I'm transported
into my dream clouds
in the hazy blue sky
where the songs
I want to hear are
being played.
Deeply inhaling
the various scents
of the still-blowing
leaves, the damp mud,
the mind boggling plethora
of blooms around me
I find myself sleepily
marching away from
reality; under the drowsy
warm gentle rays of the sun
the wind fans me
to a land far away
the words of my book
become blurry
as my eyelids
dreamily shut out

the grime and pain
of the world
i am lost for i know
not how long
and when i wake up
the leaves are long gone
snow now drapes the land
gently and harshly
no sign of the flowers
the winds now sing
a different tune
all alone
and i am now in
the winter of my life.

Temptation

Fall—your untied locks—
Temptress! do not bewitch me
Thus, I come unarmed

Dazzling decked diva
Adorned, clothed in choicest golds
I'm disarmed in awe!

I'm drawn to your charms
Like a scimitar to blood
Unquenchable thirst!

Your rustling silkens
Beckon, weaken my resolve
Eyes helplessly dart

You are all around
Smothering, blazing glory
There is no escape

But to surrender
Give in to surreal beauty
And stand wonder struck.

Rain

The sky wants to
Mirror my eyes
The clouds run awry
Like teary kaajal
The branches sway wildly
Much like windswept hair
While the rain
Washes down scents, secrets
And much-lingering memories.

Autumn Sun

Sun, o life-giver
If this is what you choose
To distance yourself from me
And move further out
Into the horizon
Then I have but little choice
To replace pain with beauty
Create a canvas so colorful
Such that it blends into
the twilight
In hues of purple, amber
crimson and citrine
And no one will ever know
The hurt I feel inside
As they marvel at the
pulchritude that is
Autumn.

Jasmine

I am the ambrosial jasmine
Coiling around vines
Dropping petals on weary travelers
Stupefying them with my fragrance
Redolent and refreshing
Truly a gift from God ;Yasmeen

Aging woods

walking into the woods
on a crisp morning
air brisk, trees blazing,
bleeding hues,
chromatic leaves
into my blood-
the weak sunshine
illuminating,
transforming my being
into an aging soul
its intense tints
penetrating my eyes;
taking me beyond
my years-
wrinkling my skin,
graying my hair,
as i nurture
and nourish the fall
in my heart
and wait for the winter
to set in.

Arrival

Skies overcast, foggy winds
arresting the wooded glen
Caged birds longing to fly
and soaking it all in,
Mountains standing blocking
the clouds warrior-like,
Enrapturing everyone
who chances to look
humans and animals alike
A throng of cuckoos and thrushes
breaking into a melody,
Rushing out as if to
escape the impending inevitable
The fragrance of the mud
stopping people in their tracks
Capturing the heart and
captivating the soul
Monsoon, spinning webs of
dreams, inspiring peacock
dances and childhood joys!

Water

Who knew
That two atoms of H
And one of O
And their ionic bonds
Could create something
So simple, so pure
So essential to life
For flora and fauna alike
Only on our home planet
And nowhere else
Cools down as ice
Warms us as vapor
Gives joy to farmers
And children alike
Cleans, moisturizes, purifies
Quenches thirst
Separates lands or surrounds them
Glistens as dew in grass
Or destroys as tsunamis in oceans
Helps navigate as rivers
Explore as seas
Beautifies as a fountain
Thrills as a waterfall
A superb creation
We should be lucky to experience!

Tide

As I walk along the wind and surf-swept shore
I pick up the soil that succumbs quietly under me
And I challenge it with a question I've never asked before
Where is your voice, dear mud?
Where is your sense of self?
Are you forever meant to bear the brunt of the tides
Or will you lash out some day and speak up for yourself?
Do you stare at the horizon, tranquil and googly-eyed
Spellbound and stunned at the spectacle before you
Such that you feel no fear, no pain, no injustice?
It says
O traveler, you need not worry for my safety
You see, La Luna and I have carefully conspired
To pull the mighty ocean towards us
And enjoy it surrender to our might unwillingly
You have it the other way around, seeker
For it is I who bears the power, and he who is powerless
In this game of tug-of-war!

Dawn

Quietly dark and then
very silently
the lambent light blushes
the sky; radiating a million
shades of rosy pink and violet,
sweeping across the horizon
like an artist's brush;
illuminating the so far
black land with a lustrous glow.
The lucent sun gradually
appears; like a newly married
bride, shy and resplendent;
ready to dazzle everyone
with her blazing refulgence;
The sparkling stars surround
her, dazed by her brilliance,
they withdraw their flashing selves
till reduced to a glimmer;
The shimmering waters reflect
her beauty and lay way for her
regal carriage;
The sparks brighten, and the
hues give way to a deep
golden ochre
The candles at home flicker out
in obeisance and the mirrors
glint in recognition;
The scintillating kiss of dawn
thus wakes up earth
from its deep slumber.

Dusk's Call

approach, wayfarer
follow my painted hues,
allow yourself to be
mesmerized by my
vibrant, florid palette
follow my silky air
rustling through the woods
like a maiden in distress
follow my bird call
chirping and twittering
in flight to get you home
follow my starlit carpets
bestrewn with gems
taking you to the queen
of the night,
follow my scented flowers
driving you insane
with their heady fragrance
follow me and let me
lead you hither
in a trance
to the unknown
where you have no
choice but to lose
yourself, enchanted—
in me.

Allure

Evening, with her dark tresses
Studded with stars
Her dark eyes rimmed with kohl
Sunset's burnished sheen
regaling her opulent cloak
of brilliant blushed silks
Pauses to regard herself
in the reflection in the
abyssal sea
gets intoxicated with
her own image,
and drifts the floral scent
of a thousand jasmines
into the wind
for all the young lovers
of the world that
become entangled in
her own bewitching allure.

Maiden

Evening, rushing to night
Proceeds to cloak your
Bashful mien with her brilliant hues
She then adorns your eager, waiting eyes
with her bright stars,
Wafts the fragrance of a thousand mogras
to the air you breathe
And rests the setting sun
on the diadem on your coif
Why would you ever need to be
swathed in silks and clad in jewels,
O fair maiden
When this enchanting ethereal evening
lavishes her beautiful splendor
On you!

Amour

Prism

After all what am I
Just an ordinary cheap piece of glass
Waiting to be kissed by your powerful rays
So I may dance in my rainbow skirt
People call me a prism
But I am merely your color-starved slave.

Balloons

My darling
I can't stand these crowds
These uniforms
Unfriendly eyes and whispering lips
I feel stripped, bare, raw and exposed
Afraid to take a turn
I don't want anyone else
But you
I don't need the friends, the social network
To be the painted butterfly
As long as I am one in your eyes
You know, you understand
You look past this gray aging tortured body
To see my colorful soul
You're the only one
That made me talk and reveal my darkest secrets
So take me away
Let's run past this society and its wagging tongues
Lay ruin to families and teachers and rules and deadlines
Let's find ourselves in green pastures and colored balloons
Cut off the harness and fly towards the sun
Let my hands be the brush and our love the palette
To stain the endless skies
This is all that keeps me alive and breathing
As I look at you
When our paths cross each morning
Then why is it
That I'm the only one left in the balloon
Where are you my love, will you not join me
Or am I to complete this masterpiece alone
With my tears and blood

Cherry Blossoms

Long walks
Around the tidal basin
You and I
Under the pink cherry blossoms
A boat ride here
Pale tissued petals in the water
Did we just meet
Or are we saying goodbye
Your eyes
Don't say much at all
Our hands
Brushing past each other
The question
Hanging above our heads
Just silence
No smiles or tears
Or long drawn sighs
Just the blazing twilight
Splashing colors on the canvas
For the next 15 days
While the pink cherry blossoms
Draw in their lovers
Until the next year
We'll always have this evening.

Roads

The road curved, lost
sight of you, but knew
you were still ahead
somewhere, followed
the sound of your feet,
the lilt of your laugh,
till it all disappeared.

Years later, it's still
searching for that
familiar face, that
smile, that wrinkled
visage, as it meanders
and culminates at
its final destination.

Ablaze

Torrid flames
Licking us clean
Sizzling to our core
Bent on scorching our souls
In the blistering heat
And for what
To rapidly extinguish
The fiery glow that
Resides within us
That makes us burn
For each other
With undying passion.
Nothing can keep us
Apart, or diminish our
Intensity, or lessen the
Incandescence of our love.
So they resorted to blind
Our dazzling splendor to
Dying embers.
But my heart,
When caste nor religion
Nor money nor class
Could tear us apart
What is a few mere
Logs of wood
How can they burn
What is impossibly
Resplendent, brilliant
Unbridled love.
Let them have their ashes
And let us have our fire.
So look at me love
Let our searing eyes burn
Forever in our hearts
Ablaze.

Crush

Of course you'll say
Its just a little crush
Forget that I've spent
My entire youth on you

Wearing your favorite colors
Singing in my best voice
Thinking that your charm
Was my only reward

That wicked gleam in your eye
That crooked smile that drove me nuts
Apparently it was meant for everyone
Not just for this hapless soul

Engaging in your witty repartee
Centered my day, my hours, my minutes
Stealing glances at you in class
Became my primary preoccupation

Now studying for an exam together
Doesn't exactly define romance
But you were equally complicit
I guess flirting was just some silly old game

Led me to believe
All this was something more
But little did I know
What lie ahead in store

It was a bloody surrender
Walked away with a ton of bruises
Pain? What's that I say
Compared to walking on shards of glass

And so it is after all
What's one more broken heart
Scattered, unclaimed
In a myriad of million such luckless tickers

Last Night (based on the movie)

Another ho-hum morning
Dirty ponytail, sweats and Starbucks
Newspaper tucked in, laces stuck out
Faced with the prospect of a weekend alone
When you show up, golden and unannounced
I blush and wish the earth would swallow me up
You're glowing, charming and devastatingly the same
And promise to call me and meet me elsewhere
I race up and still my beating heart
Take the longest ever shower, curl my hair
And put on my sapphire dress
Glittery I glide in like silk
And make you look like that again, at me
Our hearts stop and so do our breaths
As we drink in each other
Finish each other's sentences
And laugh our way through drinks
Flirtingly we tease around all evening
Till your eyes smolder and smiles cease
And then we're alone in that sea of people
Your fingers cautiously tread on mine
Burning me and spinning my head
Till I remember why we left
Till you see my wedding band
Till I force myself to recall
My better half in Philadelphia
But this is the city that never sleeps
And anything could happen
This was last night
Where will we be this morning?

Tangerine

Tangerine dreams
In shades of amber, ochre and burnished yellow
Burn in my eyes
The flame of a candle
That slow falling leaf in autumn's brilliant splendor
That full bloomed flower in your diadem
The heady fragrance of an orange grove
The citrine tint of that blessed turmeric paste
Mixed in with the clink of those aurulent jewels
Adorning your laughing visage
That glows for me
As we walk around that sacred golden fire
Beneath the caressing sunny rays
We promise never to part
Amidst toasts of honeyed tone champagne
You and Me
Our tangerine dreams.

Evening

Evening, cast its deep shadows
on us, as the sun battled the clouds
Our first meeting, in our secret spot
for years to come, with our names
etched on the tree, our hands trembling
as they accidentally brushed, me shy
as a forget-me-not, you nervous and
peering at me with those glasses, the
cuckoo that suddenly decided to sing
its beauteous melody, your adoration
laving me as the words float by me,
while the wind ruffled your bed-head,
all this and the vision of you in white
devastating me, and i crumble like sand
as the evening drew to a close, with
me tangled in the web you wove.

Abandoned

a drawer full of unopened cards
a side you never showed
unspoken words, unsaid thoughts
years of broken promises
these are some of the million
pieces you left me in
marooned on a deserted island
parched for your presence
the fire that you was
now reduced to dying embers
was it that easy to walk away
without a second glance,
to readily consent when i
told you not to come around?
how do I exist in a world
where you don't, and
is that ever going to change?
how do i bandage myself
again and make me whole?
unanswered questions, a million
of them, to keep me company
as i'm embraced by your
last gift—your abandonment.

Dry Leaf

that dried fall leaf
in my diary, crumpled
and fragile, almost in
smithereens reminds
me of a day years
ago; when i thought
i was strong enough
for the world; but it
took your deep
voice filling the
vacant and void
interstices of my being
to realize i could not
stand alone, that it took
me to say yes to complete
myself, it took your
presence to feel like a
person again, whom
love would not pass by
like it had countless
times before.

Tryst

Is this it, my love?
Fiery glances
Searing touches
Sweet passionate whispers
Fingers brushing my hair
Entreating me to stay
Eyes looking into my heart
That beats wildly for you
But knows it can not tread the line
For you are with her
And I with no one
Have we come to the point
Where the roads diverge
To remember
That two souls met unexpectedly
And now crave one another
From afar
And burn through their lives knowing
The candles share but one wick
Burn my dearest
And bid me adieu.

Marine Drive

Waves crashing ashore
On the huge pylons and rocks
The smell of sea in your hair
As we walk hand in hand
By Marine drive
The lights casting a halo
Around us as the wind
Whips through our bodies
Talking about everything
Under the moonlight
Roasted peanuts' scent
Filling the air with calm
Familiarity
Sitting down next to you
As you lean in for that
Coveted kiss
Ah what a perfect moment
A gift from the restless waters
To see young love at its zenith!

The Walk

come let us take
a walk, you and me
slip your gloved hand
into mine; and let
the desires unfurl
let the night air
waft with the fragrance
of the jasmine and fill
our beings with
rapturous delight
let the still sounds
capture the spaces
between us and resound
with our heartbeats
let the orange glow
of the October moon
cast its satiny sheen
on our eager faces
so i may regard
your perfect beauty
under its blessing
let us talk about
everything we can
or about nothing
and let our breaths
do the talking

let us take this path
lined with grass and
pebbles and stumble
and brush against
one another
let us for once forget
that though we may
always belong to one
another, the world
may not agree
come my dearest
let's take a turn
for this may be
our last.

Vision

heart aflutter
atwitter
wings on fire
each time i
set my eyes
on you
those deep
dark mesmerizing
eyes that glow
in the dark
are like a lamp
to my lost soul
those lustrous
dark locks
ravage me
make me want
to run my fingers
through them
for eternity and
pull you closer
never let you go
that twinkling
smile that speaks
unfathomable
words sending me
into a ditzy spiral
and i never want
to touch the ground
that razor sharp
brain that can
bring me to my knees

with one whiplash
who are you
magnetic one
what is this power
you wield over
a poor unsuspecting
waif like me
and why are you still
only a figment
of my imagination
what will it take
for you to incarnate
from my dreams
into reality
and sweep me off
my dawdling feet
or will you forever
just remain
that eternal flame
in my heart
no matter how much
i wrinkle and age
you always make
me feel young
so be it; may you
always be ageless
just the way you were
when i first saw you
some things are best
left unsaid, unformed
some visions are best
left untampered.

Yellow Flowers

a bouquet
of yellow roses
delivered at
my doorstep
tied with that
distinct red
ribbon took me
back to times
and places
long forgotten
when all you
had were
pennies to spend
and all i had
was my fresh
girly laughter
and the utter
carefreeness
of youth
a careless bunch
of wildflowers
brought me
as much joy
because all i
could see were
your admiring eyes
and now even if

life happens
while rushing
down on the stairs
or hastily kissing
goodbye; the flowers
are always a
beautiful sign
and reminder of
our everlasting
love.

If you were mine

If you were mine
I would not know what to do
Since that would be a miracle
I think its best I admire you
from afar
And be your own personal satellite
to reflect your glory
Just like the moon can think
the earth is hers
But the earth only belongs
to the sun . . .

The first time

that first time you
gently looked into
my eyes and spoke;
what i do not remember
since all i could do
was dumbly stare back
tongue-tied into your
molten baby blues.
you opened a floodgate
of emotions and gave
me wings that i knew
not existed. now
mornings took on a new
meaning, and mirrors
started to smile back.
and the first time you
took my hand in yours,
and my world just froze,
and then melted away
in an icy haze and i knew
not where to look, that
vein still pulsates with
your touch, in memory.

Rainy afternoons

remembering
those rain soaked moments
those gloomy days with
cloud filled skies
the anticipation of seeing
you, all wicked smiles,
teasing promises
as i would while away
my afternoons
singing to myself,
writing about you
in dim light
imagining myself
drenched in the downpour
with you
and while the world
complains about potholes
and colds and bad hair
nothing can take away
the memory of that monsoon
day with your sunbeam
kisses as rewards!

At First Sight

Bodies bumped, eyes met
Bore into each other
Stared each other down
That baritone voice
halted her en route
as she succumbed to his
reeling charms.
Emboldened by his
admiring gaze, out came
the first word, the first
conversation, and the
first date.
That's how the elevator
opened; and closed
on love at first sight.

Key

Am leaving your city
For its no longer my own
Cast myself out of it
Just like you cast me
out of your heart
That lump in my throat
prevents me from
tears soaking my hair,
the one you admired
The touch of your hands
will continue to warm
me through my cold
nights without you
As I bid adieu with a
promise to never look back,
I can't help sneaking
one last glance at your
house, where I've left my key
to a ton of happy memories,
which is all I'm taking
with me.

Head over heels

Sneaked notes on paper
Passed underneath
whispering chairs
Till they got to you
And you blushed beet
red as you tried to keep
class in order.
Playing footsie with you
under the tables as we
pretended to do our
homework, you holding
on tight to my left hand.
Not knowing what I wrote
or spoke, glowing summer
amber hued in the
exam hall, aware of fifty
pairs of eyes staring at us.
Searching for your silhouette
at the window as I sped
up the street feeling your
gaze on my feet.
Ah those were the days when
Head over heels was an
understatement.

Elemental

Burning I am
for you, how much
Fire do you need
me to show, to
prove how genuinely
I thirst for you.
Pouring I am
with every tear,
How much do
I need to bleed
to show my need
for you.
Soaring I am
with every glance
Into the wide open
sky, I can fly
I believe
to show you
my bursting heart.
Torn and thrust about
I am with every breath
With every smile
Every windswept
remark, you leave
me breathless.
But pushed back
I am, into the earth
With every smirk
with your neglect
How much do I need
to disappear, into dust
to show my angst for you.

Oct 21, 2000

That evening in October
Soothing jazz
Relieving the tension
Between us
Fingers knotting and undoing
My dupatta
Breathless glances
and shy words
Exchanging opinions
on music and architecture
and books and people
and everything under the sun
Steaming cups of mocha
Brewing silently before us
Light chatter and clinking cups
Don't break our gushing
flow of conversation
Java beans fill the air
As I pop the question
And look away
Not caring for your response
I am on cloud nine
For I have found
you, the love of my life
In this suburban Starbucks
Not knowing how the clock
spun from 4 to 8
And the stars are out
Under the cool sky
While we walk out in turmoil
Headed for sleepless nights
That magical evening in October.

Oct 22, 2000

That day in October
The light drizzle
Did not dampen our spirits
Our coordinated jackets
Kept the crisp wind at bay
The dazzling fall foliage
Wove a magical carpet
Just for us
The weak sun cast
Hints and flecks of auburn
In our hair
The brilliant tapestry
In varying shades of
Red, orange and yellow
Blinded us to the beauty
Of nature and love
Your hand touched mine
Whispers mingled
with the breeze
Your eyes sought mine
And held me captive
Hearts soared
Above all
Witnessing this moment
When we pledged
Ourselves to each other
And none else
Wildflowers bent in awe
As we gave our assent
That glorious day in October.

Unrequited

Feathery leaves of autumn
fluttering down like birds,
promising a glorious path
ahead with no misery,
as the traveler gingerly
goes down memory lane.
Waxy leaves of autumn
gathering water, like dew,
muffling their crunchy sounds,
tears mingling with the rain,
hiding from the mockery.
Charred leaves of autumn
burning auburn ablaze,
fanning the hurt,
filling it to the brim
only to pour it out in solitude.
Crumbled leaves of autumn
blackening the traveler's heart,
discarding it, suffocating and
smothering its core.
Unfinished, unrequited.

Lines

Me and you meeting midpoint
Recognizing you
In a street of millions
Our roads converging
Obscure meandering paths
Coloring our skies
With the paint of newfound love
Treading suffering
And joys with our combined strength
Seeking out our lives
In an unknown destiny
Till our hands parted
Lines on our palms straying far
Then realizing
These roads were meant to diverge
Always from the start.

Footprints

Footprints on the sand
Constant, unwavering walks
Time frozen and shelved
Waves washing ashore
Rip tides pulling us apart
Imprinting deeper
Those feet in the sandy banks
Holding on with hands entwined
Eternal togetherness
Even when the prints are gone

Senses

Like dawn you break in slumber
I'm instantly yours
Your eyes seek mine in repose
And I'm all awake
Your breath cloaks mine wantonly
I respond in kind
Your touch kindles my desire
I bloom like a bud
Your whisper sounds my sweet name
I'm carried beyond
My wild imaginations
And I'm left in vain
Your taste lingers in my mouth
Long after you've gone
Sense less though I be
My senses belong to you
Awakened, always.

Blessing

The big apple
Central park
Hushed calm
Frozen lake
Whistling wind
Under the
Snow capped trees
You and me
Trudging through
This magical
winter wonderland
Across the bridge
Hand in hand
Till we find
that golden tree
Bright with memories
and love filled
moments, as we
pause under it
and smile at the
miracle that is
our love story.

Under this very tree
where you
reciprocated my years
of devotion to you
and I could only
pinch myself
we stand again
and laugh as
the leaves empty
their snow filled
bowers on our
heads, as only
a blessing can do.

Gaze

The arrows darting fire
From your eyes
Set sight on me
And I melt
In fitting response
Taking form
To reply to those
Piercing stares
Languidly limpid
Eyes look back
Till the unshattered
Gaze is held
Captive by us
And tears blink
to threaten
its destiny
As mine close
And yours
look away
And the spell is
Broken.

Evening Lamp

Eternal glow of
The evening lamp
Suffusing your
Flushed face with
A deep calm and joy
Welcomes me every
Twilight into your
Inviting eyes
Filling my tired
World with the
Splendor of a
Starlit dusk
Wiping clean my
Slate of a million
Unworthy attempts.
The day is gone
But the night is
Still laden with
Promises.

Union

The maddening scent
Of jasmine pervading
The air with longing,
Wind filling the spaces
Between us with
Breathless heartbeats,
Eager footsteps claiming
The distances between us
Till we are one,
The magic of the evening
Enveloping us into her
Unfailing charms
And my heart knows
You are here
And will be here
Every evening.

Angst

Inkblots

Interesting
I never realized
That it could look this way too
From this angle
It does look like a secret message
A farewell to you
Can love really be condensed
Into a code
Could your thick head
Really get to the heart of it though
Would you have the patience
The sensitivity
To get to the bottom of this
Or am I to imagine
As my hand idly sketches
Its last moments
Against a mirror
Watching my life blood
Pour out of my fingers
As my eyes dimly close
And everything turns to black
Adieu my unfeeling one
Before you mop this up
Take a moment
Take a picture
Look long and hard at it
Maybe then you'll finally get
To the heart of me
Via these crimson blots and lines . . . .

Leaves

Let me just lie here
Amongst these leaves
Discarded, Forgotten
Given up for good
Let us be trampled upon,
kicked, shoved aside
for greener better specimens
that will now replace us
Let us both be carried
far away to where
no eyes can set upon us
in distaste and disgust
Let us both be swept
off the face of this earth
such that no one will
remember that we once lived.

Blue

Motionless in reams of navy satin
She lay amidst a field of cornflowers
That closely matched the sapphires in her eyes
Surrendering to the endless turquoise sky
Taking in her fill, she wandered
To the water's quietened hush
Stared at the river's cerulean depths
Felt its coolness numb her inch by inch
Until she became one with it.

That past, which once seemed so disjoint,
So meaningless, with parts adding up to nothing
With voids of vacuum interrupted by promises of normalcy
Now mattered none at all, now mingled and merged into one
Continuous stream of even dreams
Stretched into infinity.
Emerging from that macabre pain
All that remained was
One uninterrupted azure vision of beauty
Floating towards eternity.

The Room

Want to get out and explore
But the doors slam in your face
Windows of opportunity play
A cruel game of open and shut
The room grows dark
Walls close in on you
People come, stay
Then get tired and leave
No one wants to wait
Then You close the walls
And the doors and the windows
Take a deep breath and
Leave out a sigh
You think now you're safe
From the jabs of the world
Drift off into endless sleep
But when you wake up
The mirage is gone
The room is an edge
Its the tip of a precipice
Eroding with the water
The cold wind blasts in your face
Your heart caves in
The last tear gives up
And you sink and you realize
That there's no way left
To go
But down . . . .

Empty

Empty
Like I'm scooped out hollow
And filled with a loud vacuum
Resounding into open spaces
Empty
Like I'm falling off a tightrope
And the safety net has vanished
Heading for the bottomless pit
Empty
Like I'm rowing for miles
And there's no land in sight
In the vast expanse of blue
Empty
Like all the blood has been drained
Out of this vacant shell of bones
And all dreams from these eyes
Empty.

Depression

here is a
lost cause
drifting aimless
bobbing rudderless
solitary
amidst a million
faceless hapless
souls, trying to
steer clear
of the rocks of
doom, into
the vortex of
nothingness
drawn further
deeper into
the darkness
that the heart
inhabits
sinking slowly
into the murky
quagmire
of emptiness
where no limbs
can move
nothing gets
done

no person or
task holds an
iota of interest
till the mind
body and soul
all meld into one
filament of
null and void.

Petals

Petals shrug
Closing; fiercely
Guarding their
Nectar, turning
Away the invading
Droplets of the
Impending storm;
Much like my eyes
Building a fortress
For your image
Against the advancing
Army of tears.

Reverie

Evening's stark silence
Interrupts my dazed
Reverie; enormity of
Events condensed into
A single hard fact.
Leaving, taking away the
Promise of a thousand
Evenings must not be easy
And yet you did it so
Effortlessly, as leaves
Abandon their winters.
And while this evening is
Not much different with
The echoing questions about
What's for dinner and how was
Your day, now the bigger ones
Stare squarely in the face
Asking what now and where
To go from here?
Should I seek the assurance of
The black night for the chance
Of a better dawn, just as you
Have done, or is this evening to
Be my last?
Unanswered questions to which
The stars only blink back in
Unison.

Fast Food

Sometimes
There are days when
The lure of stuffing fast food
Down your throat
Is a lot more appealing
Than having your head bashed in
By your current lover
For stuffing fast food
Down your throat
There comes out that dreaded tape measure
And your traitorous weighing scale
Ready to betray you each week
And while the world laughs with festivity
Heavy blows raining on you
In a crazed rambunctious festivity of their own
Make you see colors flashing before your eyes
While you are black and blue.
And each time that beckoning ledge
Summons you with increased magnetism
What makes you you is
To ignore this midnight in your life
And take a deeply satisfying bite
Of that taco, burger, pizza
And pour your sorrows into
Your ever uncooperative waistline
Barf your inner contents
Onto your lover's narrow minded head
And run for the hills, into the midnight
Never for once, looking back.

Mirror

What say you?
To this lusterless skin
Scanty hair
Weak muscles
Parched lips
I know, you'll say
Hope is not lost
Age is just a number
You'll recommend
A hair transplant?
Plastic surgery?
A hobby?
A trainer?
But don't you get it?
Look deep
Into these desperate eyes
Devoid of all the fire
Swimming in the unfulfilled promise of youth
And even deeper
Into these dark quiet insides
Without a spark to light
Silently screaming for release
Then you'll say
Stop looking
For indeed there is no hope
Superglue can't fix what's broken beyond repair
Don't ask me for answers
Let me break
Into a million pieces with you
So we are entwined together
Glass and blood — and sweet surrender.

January 1st

It's just one of those days
Where if you stop to sit and think,
You'll be unable to move forever.

If you dare to glance at the mirror
That sorry visage will be forced to smash you.

If you pick up the phone
You can only listen and no words will come out.

If a clichéd platitude of fake concern comes your way
You just want to scream.

If you brave yourself to make a plan for the day
It will only go awry.

And while the day goes on and the world goes on
You are exactly where you were a year ago.

And when everyone has a place to go and stuff to do
Your wings are clipped and your brain is mush.

And as friends try and fit you into their busy lives
Yours stretches out before you gaping and sterile.

And what the world perceives to be strength and commitment
Is simply inertia and fear.

And in the middle of laundry and dirty dishes
You wonder what it would be like to sleep for a really long time
Or simply disappear.

Yeah a New Year isn't always all that.
And while the world makes it resolutions
Yours is simple
Just to remind yourself to stay away from the edge
Every day, every passing day, every numbing day.

So why blame April . . . when January can be so
heartless and unrelenting.

The freak's dream

O delicious little morsel,
Did you actually dream big
That you could light me from the inside
As you slide down my gullet
And sink into my adipose
You lifeless piece of heaven
You dream of secreting endorphins
In the quiet hope that it would last forever?
Did you not realize
You've been replaced
By yet another disorder
One that comes in blue and white
And connects you instantly to the world
So while I play voyeur, stalker, witty muse
You steal the only chance I have
At that elusive feeling named happiness
So take away your instant gratification tricks
And let me sweat you out
So I can get the perfect profile photo
And the world can see
How perfect my life can be
Envy me with ferocity and passion
The beautiful mask that covers
The oversized dilapidated sheath
That is Me.

Ennui

Ennui
Sinks in
Slowly, deliciously unhurried
Renders the brain comatose
Takes over a vulnerable mind
And converts it into mush
Fuses out the synapses
Numbs all sensations
Till all senses are lost
And surrendered to its mercy
Hours turn into days turn into weeks
With no end in sight
Trapped in a gilded cage
The heart forgets to scream
All energies are focused
On keeping the self tightly bound
Or else it threatens to bubble up
And explode into a quagmire
Of squelchy unmoving parts
The body soon follows suit
Into this languid state
Where the pursuer and the pursued
are immobile
Overstuffed and underworked
And longing for a marathon
Fun seems like a distant chimera
An unreachable oasis in a
Vast expanse of inactive desert
Nothing left to do
But cross each date on the calendar
Endlessly.

Daily Death

So this is how
it happens.
Every night I'm
undone
unglued
unhinged
unraveled
beyond any recognition.
Decomposed
into a million tiny molecules.
Broken and splintered
into pieces.
Torn into shreds
Every night.
The earth spins unperturbed
And with each sunrise
I painstakingly
Glue myself together
back again.
Become whole again.
Repair my wounds
and
Rearrange my visage
into a seemingly
All-knowing image
And go about my day.

Tasks, friends, my child's laughter
Usually forge my strength
While side by side
Insecurities plague me
Worries devour me
Biting tongues leach me
The world does its part
And by noon
The good and evil are equally matched.
As the clock ticks by
And exhaustion kicks in
Faith has deserted me
Hope has discarded me
And I'm left to my own devices
The gradual death begins again
Drains me of every emotion
Except despair
My soul reaches for my empty cup
And gives in to the darkness.

Suburbia

Sitting cross-legged
In my gilt castle of clutter and loneliness
Built brick by brick, panel by panel
With sweet dreams and infinite hopes
Staring glazed outside
Through the smudged windows of despair
At the strewn leaves and unearthed flower beds
Pin drop silence filling the fall air
Not a soul in sight
To beam my oft-practiced smile on
How did it come to this?
My frozen eyes can summon no tears
My leached insides can only heave a weary sigh
My muddled mind blocks and fights
Every promise-laden word
You lovingly once showered on me
The suburban dream of a bigger better life
With manicured lawns and tireless sprinklers
Has come down to
Sinkful of dirty dishes and unwashed hair
Toys, diapers and screaming cries everywhere
By princess of your heart you actually meant
Domestic goddess extraordinaire or soccer mom

Which I'm not
By staying together you meant
You with your high-flying city job
And me navigating the endless mire
Of aloof faces in tennis classes
Going at it alone
With canceled dates, solo dinners
Late nights and absent weekends
When you're supposed to be there but really not
These are
Promises, like pie-crusts, that turn sour and are easily broken.

Adieu

one mistake
treading gingerly and
broken ice
cracks under pressure
creates fissures
along the surface
rapidly spreading
much like heartache
squelches my blood
constricts my airways
and i can't breathe
avalanche
gathers momentum
pounds rocks
fiercely attacks
much like the
wintry mist of your
fading love
and rejections
defeat lingers near
clouds my vision
as i give up in despair
and let the crevasse
swallow me into the earth
as my swan song.

Winter

Winter limbs, still as ice
Poking and prodding me
As I walk along paths
Lined with your footprints
From eons ago
Trying to etch their heartbreak
Into my thick skin
And pared soul
Coaxing me to let loose
And let tears mingle with the snow
Lest I too freeze
Like my unmoved heart
That tries but tires to
Follow you after you've gone
Long ago in a stream strewn
With memories of cozy hugs
Promises and laughter
Now that winter has set in
And the smiles condense to
Foggy smoke
I trudge along no longer
Looking for you
But for myself
Lost in these quiet woods.

Warrior

What does one say to a heart
Set to cast itself on fire
Stepping into the brimstone
Of hate, judgment and sarcasm
Where does one hide
On a day of peace
To let people be
And love as they are
Instead of hunting for differences
Latch on to the similarities
And learn to bond
Over humanity, acceptance and love
But alas it is not to be expected
Weekend warriors are seldom celebrated
Let me prepare to armor myself
And return beaten, bruised and bloodied.

The Pill

Mood enhancer you scary little devil
Ready to transport this bored housewife
To worlds and places beyond her reach
Make her sing and see colors and
dance in a psychedelic Broadway musical
Keep her safely held in your clutches
But when you fret that she will leave you
You are quick to show your other side
Where dark forests grow their gnarly old roots and branches
That snake around her throat as she gasps for air
In panic that you are so easily forgotten or replaceable
You mutate and suffocate her in your druggy miasma
So each time she feels like she is at the finish line
She doesn't realize she is in a ne'er ending loop that circles
Around closer and closer to her
Doom.

Unknown Writer

disappointment
sinks in like
a knife
slowly in that
delicious sort
of way
as you see
others run ahead
of you in your
dream shaped
spaces, less though
they may be
more they are
in other ways
seeking fame, glory
and vanity
while all you want
is to escape
and retrace your
steps to that
sleepy tree trunk
coupled with
your torn tomes

quills and a ton
of imagination
running far
beyond your
wildest hopes
scribbling away
in vain
for eyes only
kind enough
to view
hoping to be
found long after
you're gone.

Missing

No I do not miss
those cliques of
annoying divas,
the ones left
untouched by the
passage of time,
yet you picked
nerdy geeky me
and watched simply
as i fell hook, line
and sinker to your
powerful allure.
No I don't miss
you trying to
transform me into
something I am not,
the days of reading
your mind, trying
to keep up with
you every second,
proving I was good
enough for you.
No I don't miss
being left out in the
dark of your secret
jokes and whispers,

especially when i
realized they were
about me, or you
watching me leave
with a broken heart.
What I do miss—is
my first love—the
old nerdy me, happy
to be me in the world
of my creation.

Failure

hurtling down
at breakneck speed
without a stopper
to a place where
no red carpet unfurls
no halo is lit
only the forgotten
exist in a sort of
unspoken way
the ones
that fell off the wagon
despite clutching on
desperately,
the ones for whom
there are no laurels
and no identity,
minds wander about
discombobulated
perusing their downfall
wrecked about in
the cut throat world
and broken down
into fragments
while their peers
rush ahead to a
destination unknown
these ones sink
further incognito
contemplating the
fiasco that is life.

For . . .

She's become a pariah
That no one will talk to
For there is no reason
Discarded like trash
Deprived of a mother's love
For it was not earned
The world wants to move on
And ignore her cries of need
For no one has time
She's become irrelevant
Washed up on the shore
For there is no momentum
There is no need for the earth
To hold burdensome people
For there is limited space
And everyone is fighting for
the same resources and glories
For what else is the point
Of going on living pointlessly
Without any human interaction
For that is equal to existing
In a zoo, eating and sleeping
And yearning for company
For that matter she might
Just simply surrender to the
Tidal forces that push her
to the brink of insanity
For what else is there
Besides routine, emptiness
And nothing to show for it?

The cut

how much time, and distance
between the blade and the skin
till the first cut deliciously sinks
and bleeds, pain bubbling forth
in your memory, in your name
reds blending with my blues
the metal delicately probing
agony-ridden veins to release
finally with a sigh of surrender
till it clatters to the ground
in a teary bloodied mixture
till i fall whispering my pleas
seeing a hazy vision of you
till it all ends in a frantic haste
and its already too late.

Revenge

come and take me
sword of revenge
have your way
slice me, hack me
into bloody pieces
take your fill
of this lazy body
prone to inertia
of this enervated mind
that defiles the very
gift of life
do away with me
pierce me, stab me
for years of neglect
ignorance and hate
for inactivity and
gluttony, for envy
and sleep, and any
other cardinal sin
let this blood wash
away these freaks
so there is some
hope of salvation
left.

Asylum

cold white walls
offer me sanctuary
from the vagaries
of the outside world
its nice here, there
are no bad days,
even if someone
comes at you with
a fist or a knife.
i'm so drugged up
that i would not know
the difference.
there are laughs,
screams, both scary
and uncontrolled
and its like a nice big
celebration of all the
unwanted unhinged
members of society.
else its quiet here
and you wonder
if you've actually
crossed over to the
other side.
everyone here is a
superstar of their
own realm and no
one tells them
otherwise.
and yes, this is where
i finally found out
that i fit in.

Alive!

Monsoon

Muddy feet and splattering gumboots
Hot chai and crispy pakoras
Power cuts and buzzing mosquitoes
Splashy puddles and clogged roads
Colorful umbrellas and frilly raincoats
Burnt corn and roasted peanuts
Crammed classrooms and half days at school
Jam-packed trains and wet notebooks
Dewy leaves and never-drying clothes
Thunder, lightning and rain-laden winds
Warm towels and warmer hugs
Monsoon and childhood, I miss you both.

Time

How did this house of crumbling mirrors and faded walls
Come upon me so fast
Rusty doors and creaking windows
Stacks of paper tied up with no purpose
Broken switches and stained utensils
These used to be someone else's diminishing youth
Termites attacking the yellowish books
Powdering them into fine dust
Leaving the bookshelves musty
That I once associated with my grandparents' house
Are now my parents'
And one day will be mine
Will I too stare at the phone that seldom rings
Or the door that no one knocks
At my gnarly nails and parched skin
With Thinning hair and fragile eyes
How did I not realize this swift passage of time
As we come so shall we leave
Loved, but ultimately vulnerable and . . . alone.

The Birthday tree

The leaves of
my life
crumbling into
tatters and new
ones springing
up fresh and
green
The roots of
my life
digging deeper
into the soil
drinking in
new experiences
and creating
faded memories
The trunk growing
and branches
fanning out
into new worlds
creating new life
and interspersed
connections
The flowers
blooming first
as buds
and bursting
into colors
as dreams take
shape
Weathering
the warm rays
of the giving sun
as well as its

harsh anger
the gentle
support of the
nourishing rain
and its torrents
of sorrow
dancing to the
uplifting breeze
and staying
strong in its
fierce gusts
of challenges
staying bare
and majestic
in survival
when the snow
drapes
enduring the loss
of its blooms
and golden mane
in autumn
but ready to
welcome
the new shoots
of hope
and blossom
with the turn
of the earth
such it is
that i turned
a corner
in the garden
of life.

A child's sky

To lose and be
lost
To soar and
vanish
To set sights
way above
the clouds
And land
upon a star
To slide
on the crescent
moon
And fly like
you'd never
fall
Childhood
exists 90%
in the sky
The earth
is but an
afterthought!

Homecoming

The flower rushed to bloom,
A splash of paint soaked
my bleak wall, a downpour
of fresh mud-scented rain
drenched the wildly swaying
palm trees dancing in frenzy,
Rainbows streaked across
the clouds stretching into
the far unknown, the skies
played my favorite music
that the birds echoed,
All this and more on the
day you came home!

Happiness

Blushing dawn
Enchanting horizon
Crashing waves
Whipping wind
Sand under my feet
Yoga on the rocks
Meditating to the east
God reveals himself
as happiness
in my heart.

Home

Weary of the Guccis and Gabbanas
Want to close my eyes
And transport my senses far away
To the scent of the damp muddy earth
Jasmine and Parijat flowers' heady perfume
Sandalwood incense wafting in the breeze
Aroma of hot tea and fresh cardamom
Fragrance of coconut hair oil
An inviting and appetizing meal
Reviving my laugh lines
Brightening my face
This must be home.

Bliss

blissful moments
futile attempts though
they may be—
scratch marks on my
ratty old writing desk
coffee growing cold
chewing the end of my
well-meaning pencil
sitting at my window
overlooking the grid
that is Manhattan
watching the leaves
turn into snowflakes
as fall turns into winter
the words flow out
of my pen and emerge
as verses
and there is nowhere
else in the world
i'd rather be;
doing nothing else!

Cake

What can be
more bliss
than sinking
my teeth into
those inches of
pure decadence
as the richness of
the cream and the
tantalizing taste
of the frosting
tickles my senses
with pure delight
not really wanting
the morsel to go
down my throat
too quickly for fear
the sensation will pass
holding it captive
in my mouth
for as long as
i possibly can
letting the divine
chocolate transport
me to places
i've never been
how can simple
things like milk
fruit, sugar do
this to a person?

this must be what
a celebration
really means
the mind and body
coming together
in a rapturous dance
as the tinkling
laughter brings
you back to
your own party
making you suspend
your sensibilities
about calories
just for the evening
and you dive in
for yet another bite
and let the saturnalia
begin yet again!

Mirth

Oops!
It happened again
That twinkle in your eye
That softening of your features
A slight tug
At the corner of your mouth
Threatening to explode
Any minute now
Widening into a smile
Then a toothy grin
And the inevitable happens
Your body swings wildly
To accompany that guffaw
Eyes closed
Fully absorbed in the moment
While your giggles take over
Every pore of your being
Reach down to the very core of you
Pull your fatigued organs
Out of their endless dull routine
And give them a taste
Of what happiness feels like
You twirl around without a care
Peals of senseless laughter
Fill your face with crow's feet
And for those precious moments
All is right with the world
As you dance wildly in amusement
Your chortles and chuckles fill the air
Infectiously convulsing all around you
And you cannot wait for the next round
To take you on the free joyride again!

The rival

Dear off late why do I feel
That we're not on an even keel
Am I not your one and only
That you welcomed so lovingly?
I can still remember your look of glee
As I was described to you so convincingly
Your fingers and toes practically curled
When I took a step into your perfect world
Yet off late I see your eyes wander
Especially at that amazing new model yonder
Your fingers don't linger on me that much
I can see who it is you yearn to touch
I barely get from you a polite hello
All I hear you do is scream and bellow
What happened to that lifetime guarantee of happiness
That made us an inseparable pair to address
Are you really that easily led astray
By that white skin and coat and promises to play
Will you so readily discard your blackberry
And sprint towards her, despite our rivalry
You broke your promise that we would be together
And got mesmerized by "someone better"
Well-played I say, she put the moves on thick
And you're not the only one to be fooled by that clique
There are millions of others wrapped up in her spell
The iphone, that fruity one has you ringing like a bell
Farewell my friend, I'd like to wish you well
But seeing you this hypnotized, I say go to hell!

Summer walk

Summers, gardenias
Walks along the pier
Dreams scattered, revealed
Fears confided, laughs exchanged
Distances collided, yet kept
Shy glances, coy smiles
Hands in my pocket
Skipping stones, singing ditties
My fair weathered companion
Till that last day of summer.

Summer evening

Lazy summer evenings
You and me on the porch
Sipping iced tea and lemonade
Talking about all in general
And nothing in particular
Remembering days like this
Long ago; when you would come by
Under the pretext of borrowing a book or a cup of coffee
Just to catch a glimpse of me
Laughing at silly jokes
Watching our paths unfurl
Till they merged as one
Reminiscing happy days
A summer wedding, multiple birthdays,
kids running around in the yard,
Fist fights, prom dates and graduations
Holding our grandchildren for the first time
And now in the winter of our lives
With rough hands and wrinkled eyes
Resting our heads on each other
Looking back at a life's work
But when I look at you
It will always be a
Summer evening.

Atoms

*

Psychedelic dreams
Taking shape before my eyes
Mundane to Sublime

*

A day passes by
Sorrow lazes in my heart
Unwieldy bubble

*

How can this rain be
Setting fire icily
My parched mind and soul

*

Light shines in my cup
My latte swirls in the sun
I love my mornings!

*

Why am I chagrined
With the storm in my teacup
The sun has spots too

*

Mothers toil and weave
Children stretch through the fabric
But it leaves no tear

*

Evening casts its
Chimeric glow on your face
Life is now complete.

*

O whispering wind
Subtly changing the landscape
You hidden artist!

*

That deep gash inside
Like fissures within the earth
Forever molten . . .

*

Youth, heady cocktail
Brash, uncaring, now bereft
Except in my head . . .

*

Rapturous feet run
Not caring which direction
Just to hear your voice

*

Ecstasy, divine
On saying your hallowed name
Tears me up with joy

*

Purple, mottled scars
Yet here I am at your door
For another chance.

*

Anklets splash gaily
Treading muddy puddles since
You came with the rain.

*

Now I bid adieu
Youth, my ever fleeting friend
Winter has begun . . .

*

The promise of youth
Bloomed and withered, left its mark
Peppered with regret.

*

Memories, crashing
Down on my rooftop like a
Lost pile of journals

*

Sometimes I wish for
Perennial amnesia
Other times its you.

*

Footsteps echoed;yours
As we said final goodbyes
Begging me to stay . . .

*

That chill in the air
Swirls its way into my lips
And frosts my tea cup.

*

Frozen brush pauses
Rests on cold painted palette
Stares at its leaf art.

*

Burnished copper sheen
Today nature has cast to
Warm this chilly earth.

*

Dreams overtake me
Fall into billowing sheets
Drag me to their depths

Sleep capsizes me
Drifts me along drowsy seas
I'm lost to the world.

*

With skillful coarse hands
Friendship, elixir of life
Intricately brewed.

*

Depositing silt
Babbling brook gurgles on by
Salt of youth lingers.

*

A hint of color
Then splashed, awash and aflame
Tree's kaleidoscope!

*

Our last rendezvous
Let words remain unspoken
Cling like that last leaf

*

Scent
of buds
Wake me up
To your hard gaze.
Your skillful magic
Claims my eyes and its light
Till we are locked in and drunk
To our intoxicating breaths
Driving us senselessly unconscious
Till we're inebriated beyond cause.

*

Tryst
With you
With the moon
as my witness
Is like walking around a sacred fire
Seven times we met in a starlit sky
Promising vows
That we would
Hence be
True.

*

Step away from the desk o pedantic soul
And admire the majesty that is autumn.
You can read about it in books and sonnets
And recite it in a voice so solemn
But unless you dance about under the trees
and step outside and breathe that crisp air
Your passion will soon dwindle fast and cheap
And your poems will soon be threadbare.

*

Mom
Let me
Be alone
On this dull day
This blanket holds more secrets than the world.

*

Drops
Fall swift
Hurt my cheek
Rainy salvo
Sharp.

*

Charred
Colors
Creator
Crafty Chroma
Canvas of Crimson and Citrine combusts.

*

The trees are ready
To shed their glossy coiffure
The earth is reborn!

*

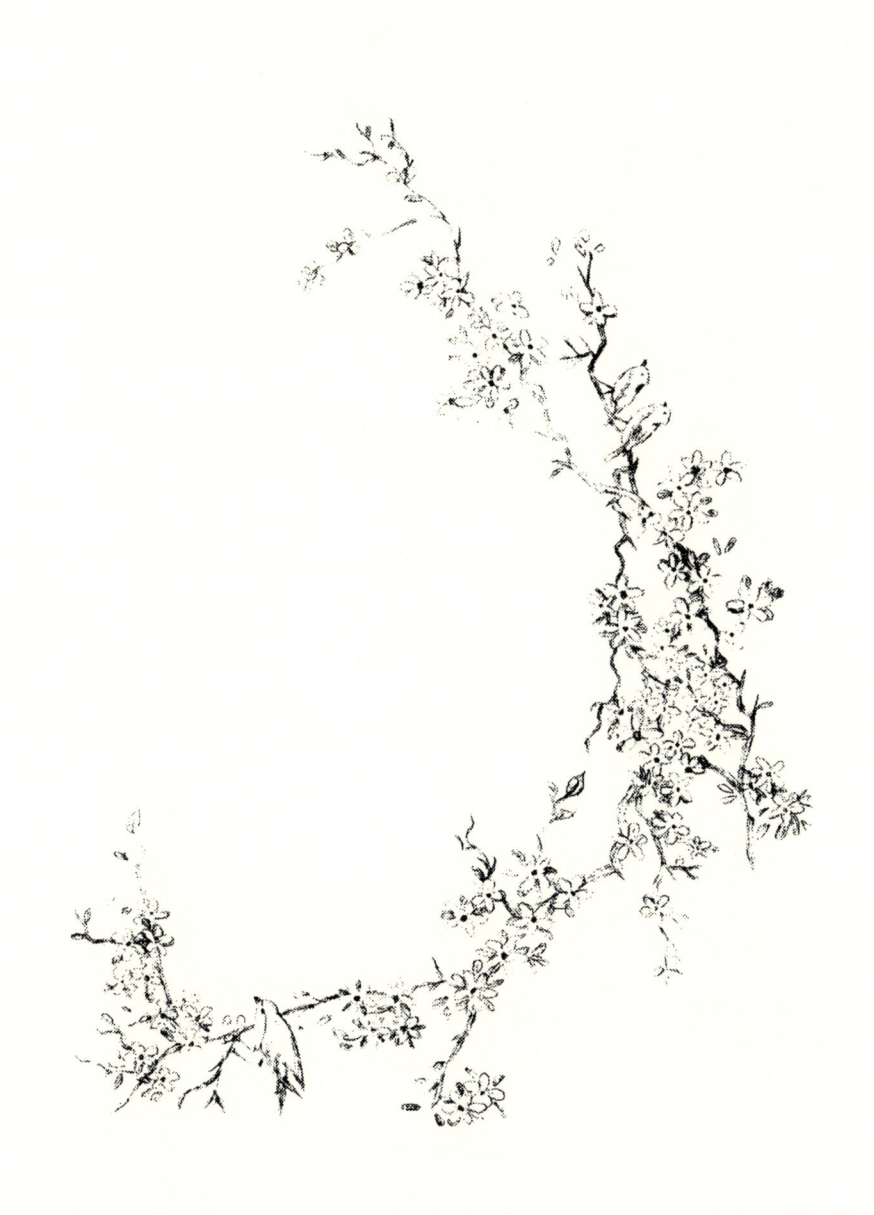

Credits

My husband *Nitin Mahadev*, for being my friend, philosopher and guide and most importantly, editor and first reviewer of this book!

Deepa Sundararaman, for her eloquent and heartfelt foreword.

My mom, *Kamala Hariharan*, for her sketch for the Atoms section.

My sister, *Aparna Hariharan*, for the finale sketch.

My cousin sister-in-law, *Priya Shankar*, for her sketch for the Awe section.

&

The one and only *Indu Vaidya*, for her sketches for the Angst, Amour and Alive sections.

Special Thanks to

Shaheen Malik, for goading me to write this book, and for her awesome publicity video!

Vineeta Chopra, for her soulful narration of a favorite poem.

Shilpa Shah, author of a *Few Joys Bunched Up* for her prompt and sincere help.

Vijay and Priya Fafat, for their encouragement and support.